sexy

hiking

man

sexy

/ˈsɛksi/

Saznajte kako izgovarati

adjective

    1. 1.

    sexually attractive or exciting.

    "sexy French underwear"

sinonimi:

sexually attractive, seductive, desirable, alluring, inviting, sensual, sultry, slinky, provocative, tempting, tantalizing; nubile, voluptuous, shapely, luscious, lush;

feline;

bedroom;

flirtatious, coquettish;

*informal*hot, fanciable, beddable, come-hither, come-to-bed;

*informal*fit, peng;

*informal*foxy, cute, bootylicious;

*informal*spunky;

*vulgar slang*fuck-me

"she's so sexy"

erotic, arousing, exciting, stimulating, hot;

sexually explicit, titillating, suggestive, racy, risqué, provocative, spicy, juicy, adult, X-rated;

rude, coarse, smutty, pornographic, vulgar, crude, lewd, lubricious;

*informal*raunchy, steamy, naughty, horny, porno, blue, skin;

*informal*saucy, fruity;

*informal*gamy

"a TV show featuring sexy home videos"

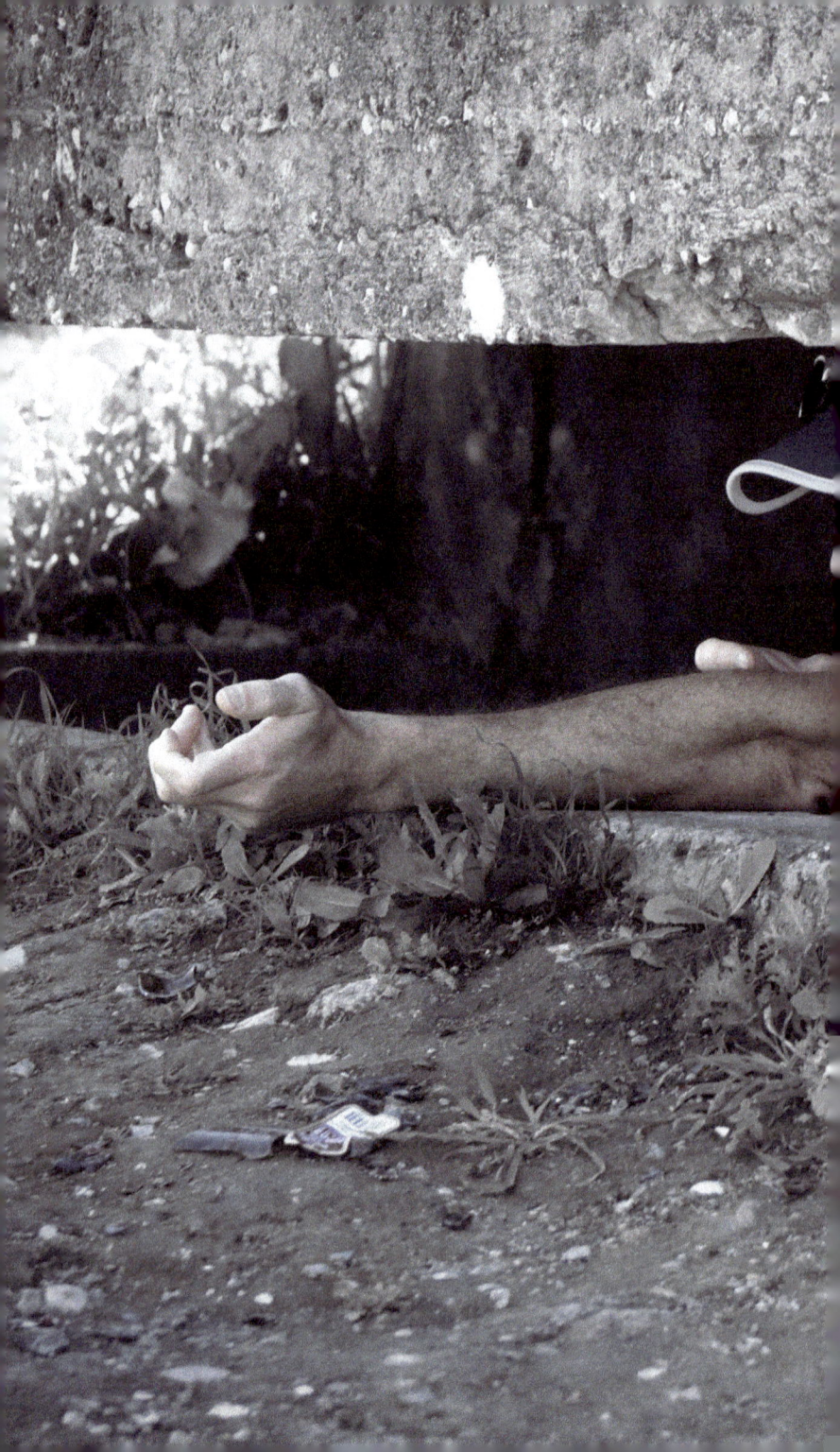

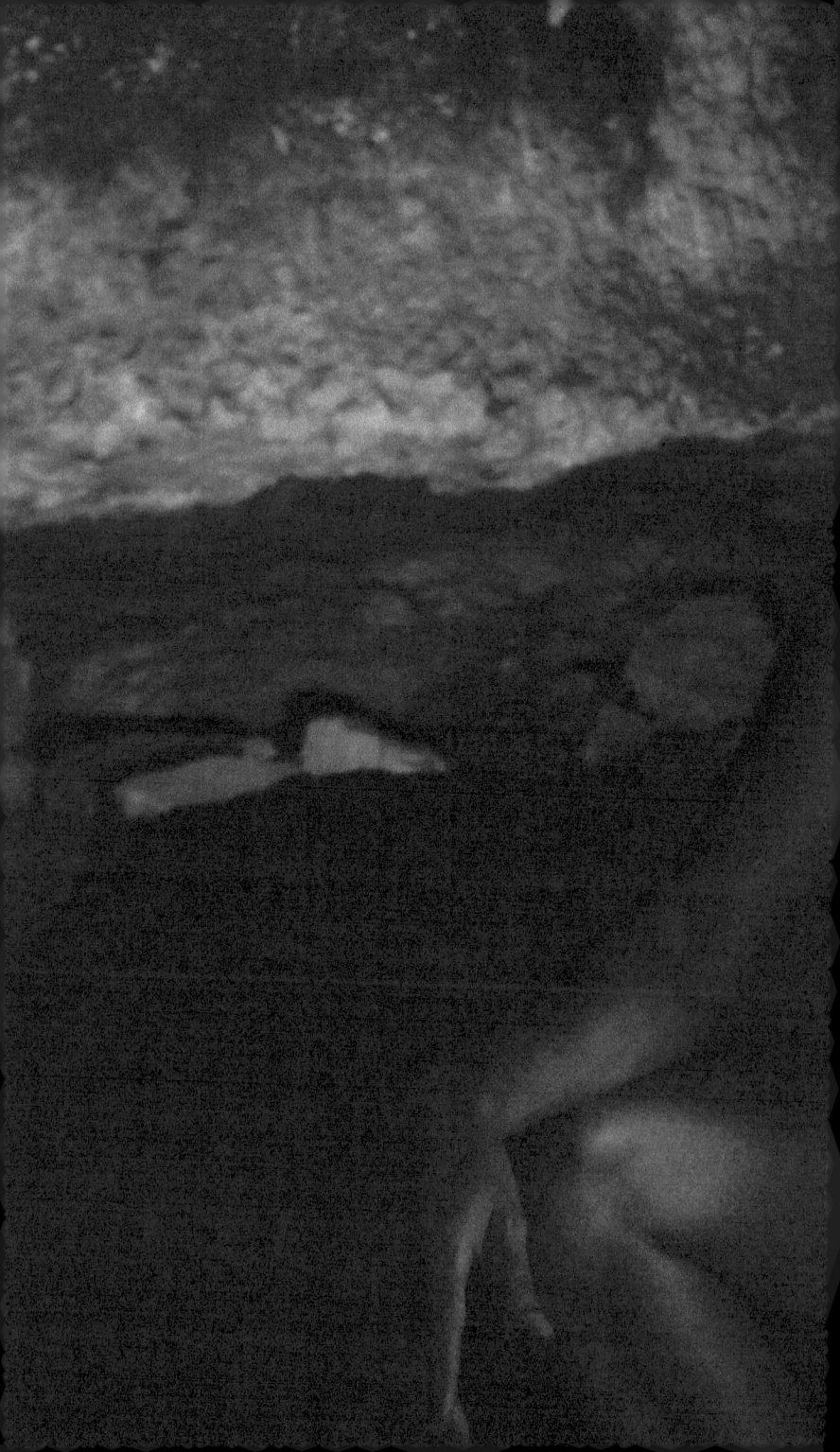

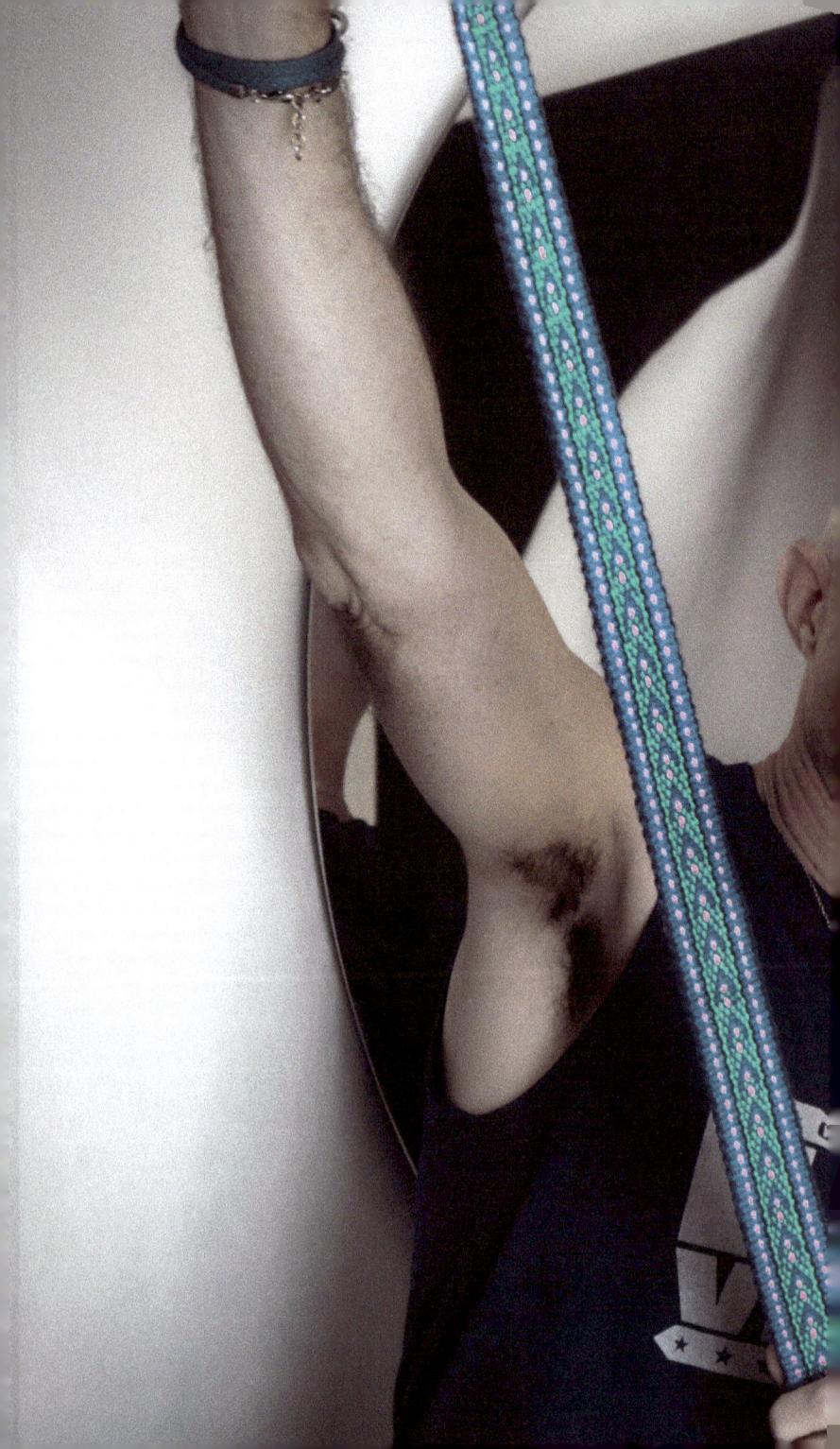

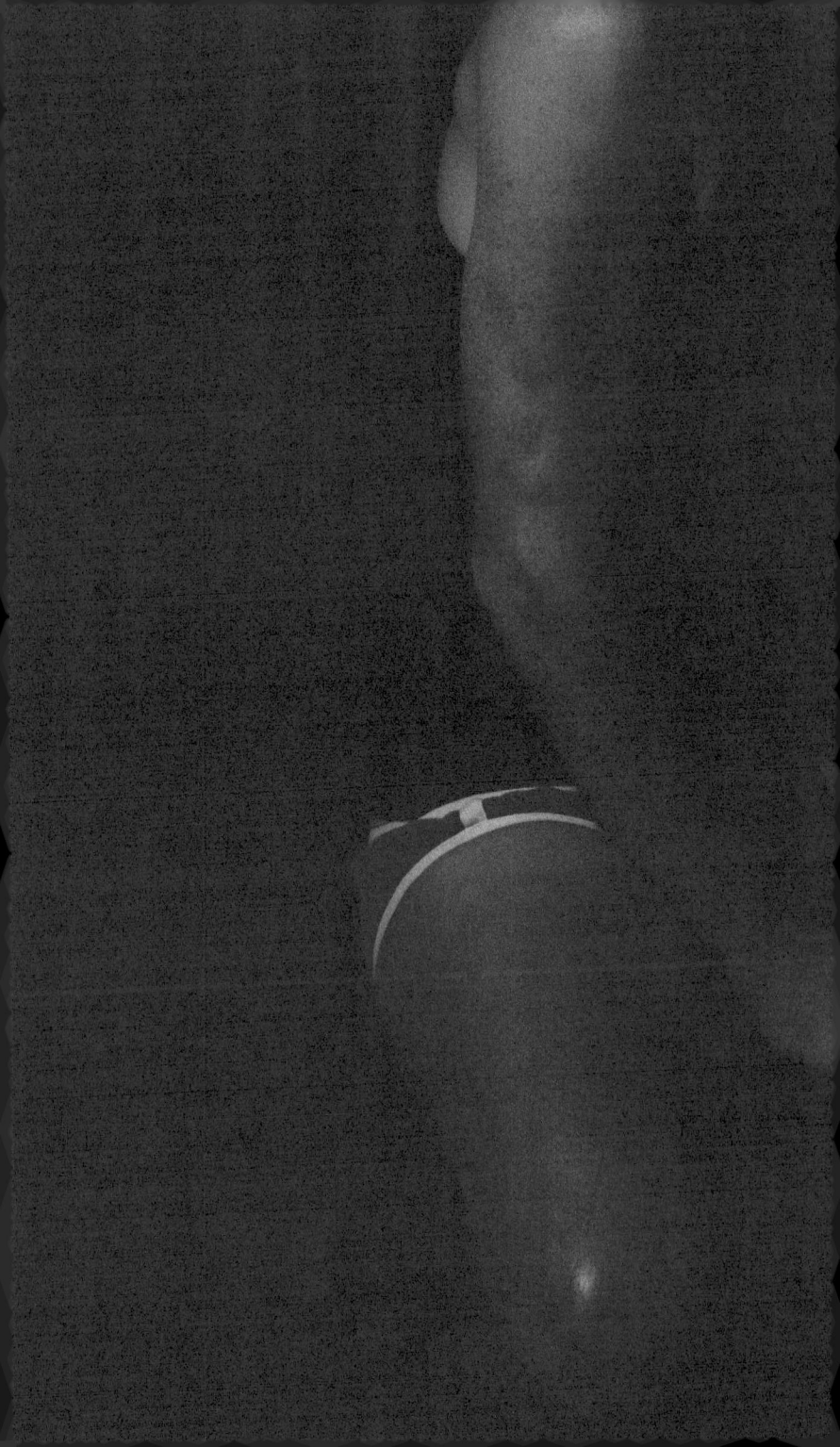

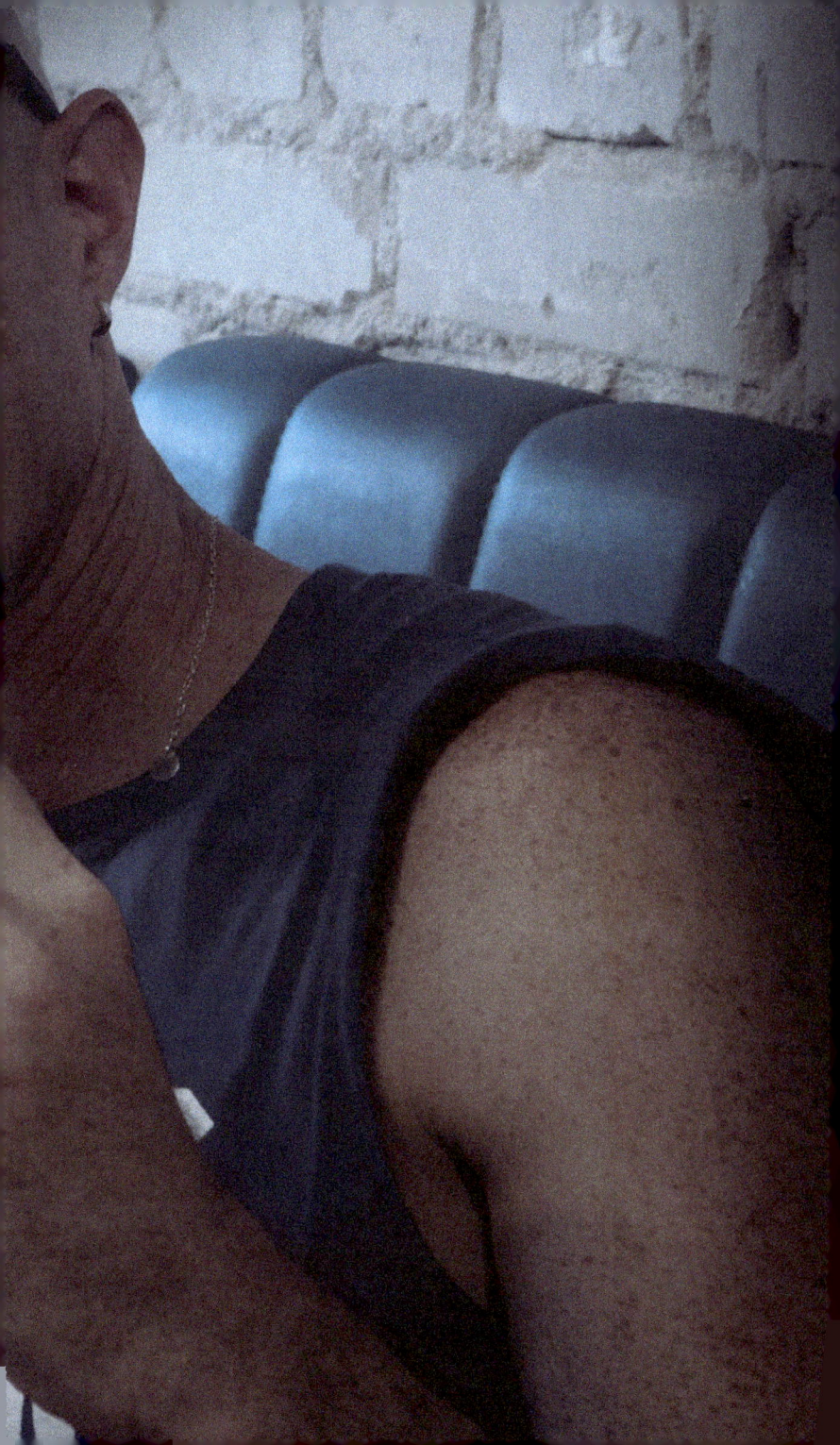

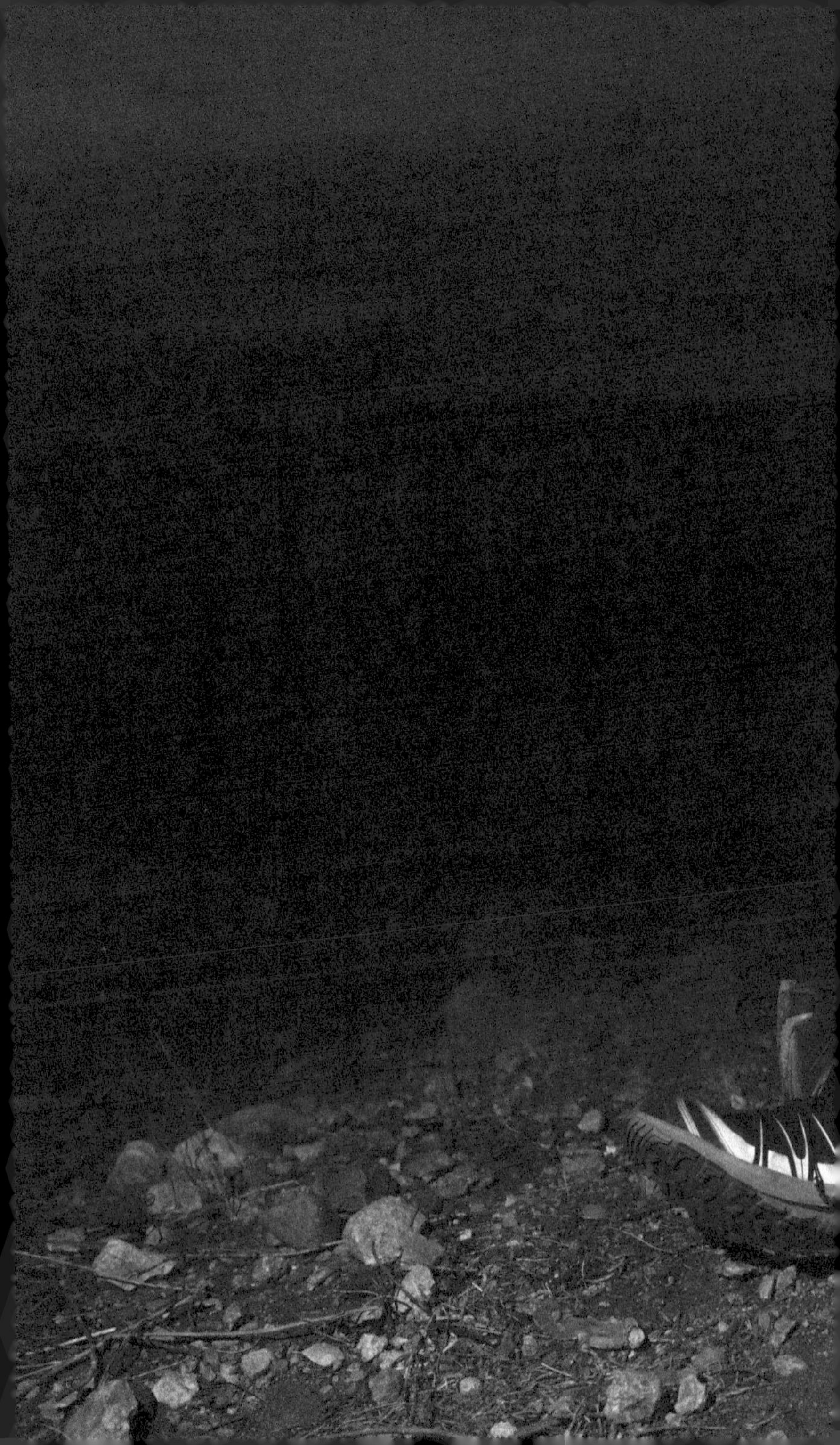

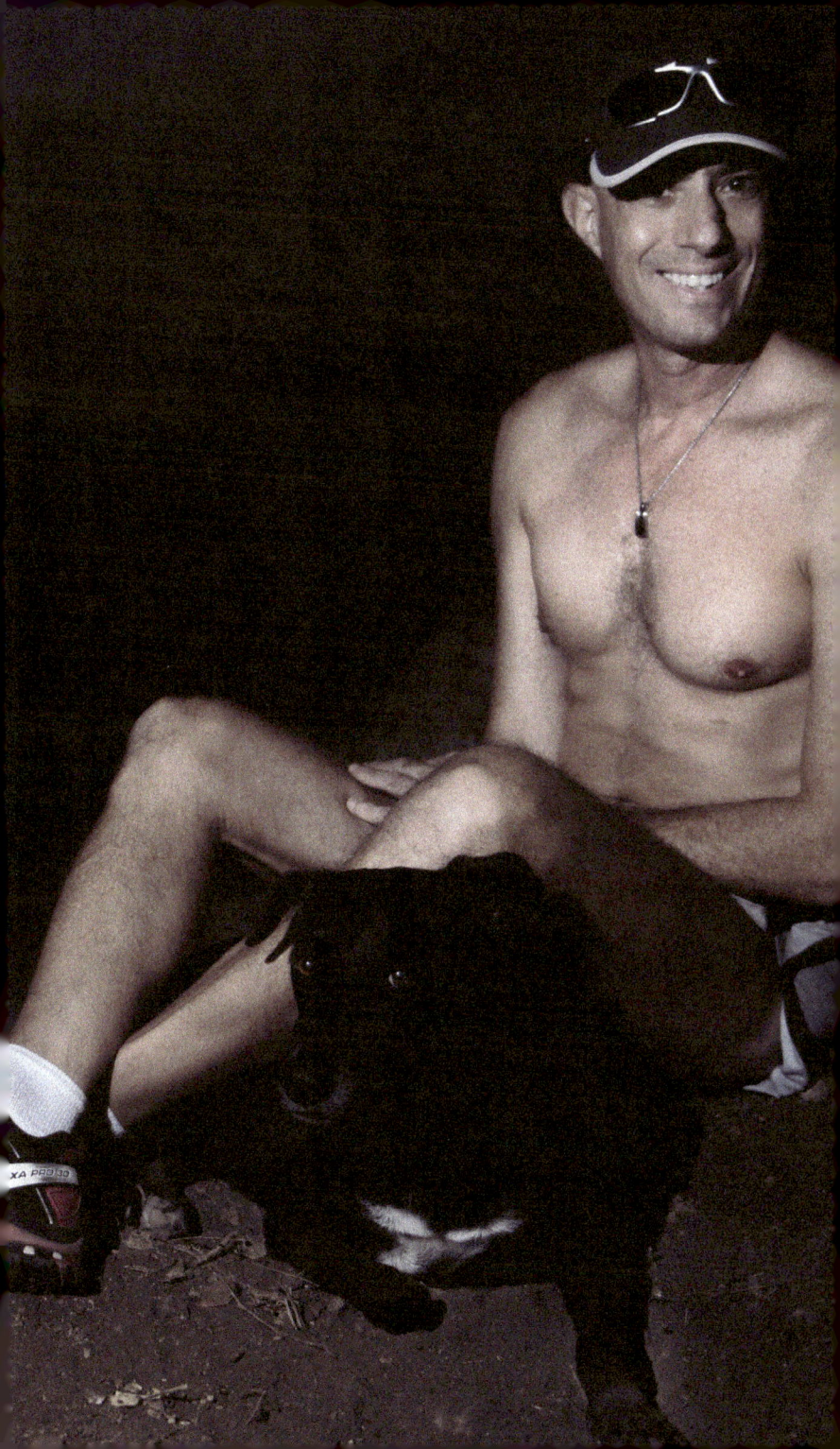

CPSIA information can be obtained
at www.ICGtesting.com
Printed in the USA
BVHW022001280719
554531BV00010B/294/P

9 780464 095958